Spells & Other Ways of Flying

Spells & Other Ways of Flying

Poems by

Barbra Nightingale

© 2021 Barbra Nightingale. All rights reserved.
This material may not be reproduced in any form, published,
reprinted, recorded, performed, broadcast,
rewritten or redistributed without
the explicit permission of Barbra Nightingale.
All such actions are strictly prohibited by law.

Cover art by Cesar Levy
"Reike Goddess" (acrylic on canvas)

Cover design by Shay Culligan

ISBN: 978-1-954353-46-6

Kelsay Books
502 South 1040 East, A-119
American Fork, Utah, 84003

For Joshua, always

Acknowledgments

Grateful thanks are given to the following journals where some of these poems first appeared or are forthcoming, sometimes in different forms:

Apalachee Review: "Faith"
Calyx: "Dance Without Sleeping"
Crit Journal: "The Unfair Sex," "Making Something Out of Nothing"
Cumberlands Poetry Review: "Miranda's Fairy Tale"
Droplet: "Miranda Goes into Hibernation"
Fourteen Hills: "The Cape Was Never White"
Gargoyle: "Ahab's Second Wife"
Georgetown Review: "Science and Sex"
Grabbed Anthology, Beacon Press: "Redemption"
Jet Fuel Review: "Aligning Our Chakras"
Kalliope: "Miranda in her First Short Poem"
Lummox Press: "Wolf Moon," "Cold Front in Miami"
MiPoesis: "Romancing the Numbers," "The Art of Removal"
Mississippi Review: "Mountain Reel"
Narrative Magazine: "Perhaps an Albatross," "Take it on a Wing"
Night Picnic Press: "A Parliament of Owls," "A Descent of Woodpeckers," "A Murder of Crows," "An Unkindness of Ravens," "A Flamboyance of Flamingoes," "An Asylum of Cuckoos," "A Murmuration of Starlings," "A Quarrel of Sparrows," "A Squad of Pelicans," "A Covey of Partridges"
North of Oxford: "Granny's Guide to the Galaxy"
Pacific Poetry: "The Not So Distant Future," "Millennials"
Poetry Bay: "Commerce with the Enemy," "Some Girl Named Natasha"
Pudding: "Bending with the Light"
Rattle: "My Daughter Calls Me Hag"
RiverSedge: "What a World"
Sanctuary: "Redshift," "The Weight of it All"
Screw Iowa: "Matters of Weight"

Southern Gothic: "Charades"
Southern Women's Review: "Cold Front in Miami"
Swimm: "When Mars is Aligned"
Tertulia Magazine: "Cliches and Contradictions"
The Best of Tigertail, 2007: "The Irresistible Force"
Tigertail Productions: South Florida Anthology: "The Irresistible Force"
Tigertail; A South Florida Poetry Annual: "Mountain Reel"
Universal Oneness: An Anthology of Magnum Opus Poems from around the World: "Ghazal for My Daughter"
Urban Spaghetti: "Miranda Confesses Idolatry"
Visions International: "Sound Over Sense"

To all my fellow poets and workshoppers: A huge thank you for your kindness, courtesy, enthusiasm, encouragement, and serious skills. Without you, none of this is possible. Particularly aimed at my "Zoomers." You know who you are.

Contents

I: Incantation

Ghazal for My Daughter	15
After Auschwitz	16
Four Chords of a Broken Heart	17
Cold Front in Miami	18
Falling from the Sky	19
Matters of Weight	20
Atonement	21
Granny's Guide to the Galaxy	22
Parting Gifts	23
The (Un)Fair Sex	24
Gluttony	25
Imaginary Numbers	26
Redshift	27
Into the Fire	28
Some Girl Named Natasha	29
Un-hexing a Hex	30
Science and Sex	31
Lessons	32
What a World . . .	33
Declarations	34
When Mars is Aligned	35
Aligning Our Chakras	36
Death Isn't the Issue	39
The Lexicon of Finance	40
My Daughter Calls Me Hag	42
Clichés and Other Theoretical Truths	43
Scheherazade	44
Tonight, I Dream	46
Song of the Mattress	47

Wolf Moon	48
Picking Your Gene Pool	49
The Weight of It All	50
Faith	51
Transformations	52
Being the Man	53
Hunger	54
Not Only a Hurricane	55
Take It On a Wing	56
"Nothing Fits the Body So Well as Water"	57
Redemption	58
Six Poems from the Tang	59

II. Speaking in Tongues

The Cape Was Never White	63
Mrs. Sprat	64
Ahab's Second Wife	65
Sound Over Sense: Miranda's Crisis with Words	66
Miranda's Fairy Tale	67
Coming to Terms	68
Miranda in Her First Short Poem	69
"Dance Without Sleeping"	70
Permeable Truths	71
Miranda Confesses Idolatry	72
Miranda Contemplates Silence	73
Miranda as Mermaid	74
Pondering Stones and Their Relation to Mathematics	76
Seance	77
Contemplating Kafka and the Fate of Gregor	78
Romancing the Numbers	80

III. An Asylum of Cuckoos

A Tidings of Magpies	83
A Waddle of Penguins	84
A Parliament of Owls	85
A Descent of Woodpeckers	86
A Murder of Crows	88
An Unkindness of Ravens	89
A Flamboyance of Flamingoes	90
An Asylum of Cuckoos	91
A Wake of Vultures	92
A Mob of Emus	93
A Murmurration of Starlings	94
A Kettle of Hawks	95
A Skein of Geese	96
A Quarrel of Sparrows	97
A Squad of Pelicans	98
A Deceit of Lapwings	99
A Charm of Finches	100
A Scold of Jays	101
A Piteousness of Doves	102
A Herd of Cranes	103
A Pandemonium of Parrots	104
A Watch of Nightingales	105

I: Incantation

Ghazal for My Daughter

Each time we speak, my daughter
and I, atoms explode in my daughter.
There seems to be nothing I can do
nothing to say, nothing to save my daughter.
If I gave her the trees, she'd want the sky,
so great is the hunger of my daughter.
Words are waves eroding rock
over time, everything breaks my daughter.
Somehow, it's always my fault, still
my fault for not living only for my daughter.
The sun shines steady every day
but the moon waxes and wanes in my daughter.
Too strong, she says, too harsh, this sun, this
mother which warms then burns my daughter.

After Auschwitz

Call me heartless.
I was there and did not cry.
I did not look upon the stones
or along the walls for blood
that might match mine.
I did not hide inside
the shadows waiting to hear
a whisper of my name.

Call me heretic.
I did not cry for mercy
or an answer.
There was no One to beg,
the halls and barracks,
chambers and ovens now empty
as they weren't back then—
when everyone was burning.

Four Chords of a Broken Heart

Here is a book
and here is its cover.
Inside is gouged out.
A good place to hide.

***

See Spot run.
See Sally run.
Run, run, run.
Will you ever come back?

***

Watching you build
sandcastles decorated
with shells, I could
almost see the rooms inside,
the doors to nowhere.

***

When I was you
and you were me,
I never dreamed
it would be like this.

Cold Front in Miami

No snow like back in '77
but it rained iguanas,
dropping like icicles from trees,
their catatonic bodies too cold to grip,
falling from mango, ficus, cabbage palm,
the hibiscus turned inward and brown,
bromeliads dried up on the spot, wind
sucked them dry, even the fish turned belly up
and vultures circled the bridges, perching
with the pelicans, who warily moved over.
The longest cold front in memory,
a world gone crazy with Floridians
bundled in scarves, coats, mittens,
extra blankets piled on the bed, reading
of earthquakes, landslides, blizzards.
Everyone still waiting for a sign.

Falling from the Sky

They hiss as they're torn from the night
like skin from a thumb,
close to the cuticle, close enough
it bleeds. You stick your thumb
in your mouth, suck
the dim memory of childhood
from falling stars, the brilliance
of their birth, the silence of their deaths.

Look at the dazzle, this sparkling
canopy, an eloquent mystery,
the movement of the galaxy
a constant, the zodiac fixed
like an old friend, a symbol
of times gone by, where once you knew
what you were just by looking
at the night sky or reading charts,
as if it could ever have been
that simple.

Lines from a fortune cookie:
You will meet a tall, dark stranger.
Look into your cup: tea leaves are curling.

Matters of Weight

I could pour out my heart
but nothing will hold it,
not the river running
without looking back
or the ocean rushing to spill
itself on foreign lands.
Nothing would keep it
from rolling like a boulder
gathering more and more mass
as everything it passed
became part of itself,
the thick, loamy smell of it,
the heat so hot it's cold,
or the chill so cold it's hot.
Nothing would stop it
but the laws of velocity:
a wall, a phone call from the past,
the prayers of your children
that morning—till body slammed
backward, then forward like a fish
on a dock, stopped cold, stopped short,
as if you could never climb the rail,
never stand toe to toe,
never look that butcher in the eye
above the glass cases—stopped.
Finally. Forever.
As if forever were a place
you could finally rest.

Atonement

Of course, it comes to this:
me asking forgiveness,
having spent my life knowing
it all, my bullish self-assuredness,
my rough-edged-ways,
my pure gift for exasperation.
Now past my own zenith,
the wisdom of being a fool
laid upon my shoulders
like a hand-knitted shawl,
I can say to you both: Father,
Mother, who had to endure
one without the other, yes,
it is true: you are smarter
and stronger and braver
for having lived through us all.
Tell me, what good that knowledge
does you now? Where in the cold, dark
of eternity are you listening?

Granny's Guide to the Galaxy

On nights when Florida pours herself
like molten sky into the darkness,
when breathing feels like drowning
and no one wants to swim through the night
to sit by your side, it might not be
the best idea to drop a hit of acid,
then ask your grandmother
how to clean puke from the wooden floor,
or tell her at length how you and the family cat
have "exchanged consciousness"
and now are both one and the same.
You might *not* want to tell her you're "tripping balls,"
that the intensity of color, the liquid brown
of the cat's eyes, the feel of the fur
beneath your hands made you want to weep,
though she did clean up the vomit,
make you a cup of chamomile tea,
wrap you in a soft blanket against the chills,
and sing you to sleep when just the thrill
of unfolding your limbs
into a run, or climbing to the top of a tree
was as high as you wanted to be.

Parting Gifts

I give you the taste of bile stinging my throat
each time I close my eyes to sleep,
the smell of dead rats on the things I had to bring home,
the sound of your blood dropping from room to room
till it pooled into gel on the bedroom floor,
the image flash burned onto my eyes, how you
corkscrewed your arms, hammer clawed your knees,
the maggots in what was left of your nose.
This is the last gift you gave to me. I give it back.

The (Un)Fair Sex

They say the sins of the father
visit the sons, but they
don't know women
have more powerful ghosts,
secrets emblazoned deeper
than letters carved in red,
secrets better left hidden
to smolder and flare,
secrets when raked over coals
burn hotter and longer
than the last "I'm sorry"
you'll ever say.

Gluttony

There is a worm in my heart
working its way through empty chambers
having fed its fill on my rich, red blood.
Knowing no restraint, it saved nothing,
and now crawls mournfully, scraping
long, hollow trails going nowhere.
Soon even the muscle will be gone,
leaving only the gristle
which even the hungry worm
cannot chew and then, feeling nothing,
it will not matter what I thought I knew.

Imaginary Numbers

It's not about the books read or the meals
eaten or the places traveled or the fights
blistered and forgotten; it's not
about the friends made and lost,
the clothes bought and worn, the cars
driven to the ground or not, the love
made or just used up.
It's not about the time that's passed
or the time that's left; in years it sounds fleeting
but in days 24,090 seems like a lot,
and 7,300 left seems longer than 20 years
and a lifetime of 32,000 give or take
seems like it ought to be enough—
until it's not.

Redshift*

For Joshua

Science states parallel lines do not intersect,
yet over the years, we have crossed paths
like swords in arms—combative, yes, but just
as often comradely, collusion and collision so similar,
as you spin off in your own orbit toward the future,
unknowable, mysterious, revealed only to psychics
attuned to the signs, while I, ignorant
and soon to be alone, can only wait for the "truth foretold,"
can only hope you have the tools to build
whatever you need for whatever storm will come.

* A redshift occurs whenever a light source moves away from an observer.

Into the Fire

Into my cup a bitter brew,
a dash of spite, splash
of rue, steaming tears.
Who am I kidding?
Witches don't cry
but snitches do.
Wolf! Wolf!
Little Boy Blue.
Little Girl Red.
Counting the days,
Sheep in the deep.
Where sleeps Little Bo Peep?

Some Girl Named Natasha

You hear the name and right away
You feel snow and fur caps
Pulled over long, dark hair,
A foreign accent and lonesome
Miles of tundra, barren and cold.
You listen to the story and your breath
Comes out white clouds of frost.
You can't imagine the innocence,
The heartbreak in being naive,
And you want desperately
A happy ending, a Bullwinkle
Come to the rescue, but not this,
This boy standing before you,
This one so earnestly preaching
The virtues of giving to friends
In need, answering the call
With the last of his summer money.
You know then and there he's just a boy
With a moose of a heart, and secretly,
Oh so secretly, you're glad he is what he is.
Not a Boris in sight.

Un-hexing a Hex

First, she says, *I need a name,*
then a birthdate. A photo, too.
I look around the room. No ball.
Crystals, yes. Amethyst, sparkling
in late sun, a candle or two.
Very pretty woman, still young,
no need for shawls or scarves.
She says no silver will cross her palms.
PayPal will do nicely, thank you.
Tomorrow we begin.
The room is darkened, candles burn.
So does the photo, the name and date.
I shudder in the non-chill non-breeze
of a nervous thought: *Do I dare
disturb the universe?*
Too late! The deed is done.
Gone up in smoke. Purple, not black.
Don't worry, she assures me,
the hex will melt away; he will return.
And that's when the real trouble starts.

Science and Sex

What of the world of Quantum Physics,
atoms and quarks, electrons,
particles, waves, and beams of light.
A flash is blue, bright cerulean blue
in a tundra of white, crystal hard.
Not many have seen it
and those that have, have names
like Newton or Galileo, even Edison,
perhaps now Gates, moving
from electron to silicon.
Perhaps this explains
how, untouched, I still yearn
for the excited rubbing of atoms—
yours against mine,
any you, any how,
as long as there are eyes
to look into, perhaps to swim,
perhaps to drown.

Lessons

In our 60s and 70s one would hardly think
such lessons necessary; however,
women of a certain age don't know
the tools available at any local shop
specializing in pleasure, and so
a trip, a research mission
is inevitable, laughing shyly
among the aisles, nervously looking
over our shoulders, under the displays
for hidden gestures, shop girls laughing
as we ogle the aisles, our purchases
made with giddy exuberance
and a keen desire to be alone.

What a World . . .

So this doctor says vaginal stimulation is essential in an unknowable way to bladder health, and now there's even a home tens-like unit one can buy that will simulate (or is it stimulate?) the physical therapy you've been having where the tech shoves three fingers inside and says "squeeze and hold" while this machine you're wired to says "work!" which means the same thing as "Squeeze" only doesn't sound quite so provocative, as if watching a graph of your muscles contracting while someone's hands are in your vagina, and another probe is up your butt, could possibly be even remotely misconstrued, especially given the small, cold room, the table and metal stirrups, the crackly thin, paper beneath you, but you think, "what the hell—most fun I've had in years!" and turn your head to watch the graph steadily falling as the seconds tick by.

Declarations

My mother says I've lost my sense of humor.
You say I've lost my *joie de vivre*.
That last lover broke me,
the pieces scattered to hell
never came back.
I expect them to show up any day now,
begging to be put back in place.
Self-fulfilling prophecies are all the rage.
Better get yours before they run out.
We will play Scrabble or Mahjong
while we are waiting.
I will cheat and you will accuse.
We will both be right.
I'm digging my way to China.
Come join me.
Every now and then it's necessary
to just get down and dirty.

When Mars is Aligned

And the moon is in its second house
or is it third? Or fourth or fifth?
I can't keep track of all those lyrics
let alone events the symbols might portend.
The only thing I'm sure of is the night sky
and how when I look up in the dark
I see the red planet winking,
the moon going through its phases,
the planets moving together or apart.
What would Galileo say about the galaxies
twisting and turning in space,
the bubbles and black holes, the dark and heavy
matter pressing down on all the souls of earth?
What would be the point, he'd say,
or maybe what difference would it make?
One way or the other, we're collapsing
on ourselves, the seas are rising,
and each breath we take is measured.

Aligning Our Chakras

in collaboration with Denise Duhamel

Root

I have a red dot that looks like a penny.
It may not seem like much but
it's the beginning—this coin is the seed
of my spirituality. Pound for pound
the scales will balance. As I roller skate
around your aura, the ground
comes up to meet me: fearlessly I bounce
like a quarter off a perfectly made bed.

Sacral

My navel attached me to my mother, led me
to a new world where I was more
than just an apple or orange. In this hybrid experience
I could be grafted into a new breed,
a poet/racecar driver/cosmetologist.
I could write with six arms, my engine purring,
my hair blower mouth puffing
"Ready. Set. Go!" A checkered flag
drops. Sonnets billow
from my tailpipe, drift to the clouds.

Solar Plexus

I have a squishy core, like jelly in a donut.
Take a bite. It's good, right?
The earth keeps its magma under wraps
until it bubbles to the surface with an "oomph!"
How much of our lives can we truly control?
Breathe in. Breathe out. Chant ohms.

Heart

My heart is locked—yours has the key.
Together our colors bloom on the wall
like these paint samples, little bookmarks
of sapphire and antique white.
Can we remodel our hearts?
Mine feels a lot like Formica.
Yours, a plush throw pillow.
It's a new life—let's go.

Throat

Sometimes I say "Great" when I mean "Uh oh,"
a sob caught in my throat like a stick
turned sideways. My dog loves to fetch,
even after I'm tired. I could cough it loose,
but where would it go? My poor puppy
doesn't know why I'm screaming.
Now the stick's gone, I miss it.
I climb the fence into my neighbor's yard.

Third Eye

Imagine Cyclops with three eyes
or me, at thirteen, a pimple
in the middle of my forehead. Who could love
someone who sees so much? Can the one
who sees everything love herself?
An empty mirror is a dangerous thing.
A vain queen gone—poof! An opaque ghost.
Still, nothing is ever erased.

Crown

My fontanel is fully closed
like a moon roof. I might start climbing
the stairs to heaven, Led Zeppelin in my earbuds,
a rosary around my wrist
or stay grounded, a lighthouse beacon
pulsing onto rocks, mermaids and mermen
with tangled hair. The sirens are singing in my head.
Sweet chorus open my spirit.

Death Isn't the Issue

What? Did you think life
was an infinite adventure?
The endless loop icon
an actual representation?
Hey buddy, no one, I mean
no one, gets out alive.
Sure, we can postulate theory,
cite Nostradamus, Houdini,
imagine breaking out
of trunks, water tanks, straight-
jackets right out of our nightmares,
but the truth is, no
one has ever made a case
for life everlasting, vampirism,
of course, notwithstanding.
Blood was never my drink of choice,
however much I like red wine.

The Lexicon of Finance

A new language has entered my house
from the mouth of a 25-year-old
I've known all his life.
He speaks of calculated risks
and stop orders, cryptocurrency
and market shares.
He tries to explain Block chains
but all I can vision is the daisy necklace
I made as a child, wearing them
on my head till they shriveled and fell off.
Investing is like that, too, he says,
excited with his newfound passion.
I hear him debating dividends
versus reinvestment, buying low,
selling when it rises, buying again,
selling for much, much more.
He and a buddy talk about active markets
and strategies and the closing bell.
There are adjustable rates
and additional hedges, AGIs and APVs,
affirmative obligations and after-hours trades.
Anticipation, arbitrage and algorithms,
and those are just a few of the "A's"!
They go on and on till the close of day.
He's studying not to be an "Aunt Millie."
There are backups and Barefoot Investors,
bears and bulls and raids and calls and puts.
To hear the talk you'd think them budding
wolves on Wall Street, but these guys
have their ethics, opportunity's their biggest thrill.
Today's task is a calculated stop order
as he consults his gurus, whomever
they may be, excited at last to wake up the next day.

As for me, cajoled out of a modest sum,
I'm happy to see him testing his limits
growing (or losing) as we both age up
(and possibly out) of this ticker-tape life.
Pride is not a word I found in their mouths,
but it's one of the juiciest in mine.

My Daughter Calls Me Hag

then the B-word, followed
by the C-word just before—
or is it after
I boiled her in oil, stewed
her up in a bowl served to her father?
That's one version.
Another says it's smoke and mirrors,
a classic pull-the-wool-
and-be-done-with-it story
straight from no one's mouth
tasting of nothing like truth.
But so it goes: her version,
my version,
the version before the sky fell,
the one before that, and at least
two or three that happened after.
I sit at my loom, counting stitches.
When I run out of numbers
perhaps I'll understand
how we came to this:
bone in our teeth,
gums dripping blood.

Clichés and Other Theoretical Truths

"Not all who wander are lost."
—J.R.R. Tolkien

Can't see the forest for the trees?
Seek and ye shall find.
Leave no stone unturned.
There's a needle in that haystack:
start sifting and it will surely
prick your finger, leave a trail
of blood only the dogs can smell.
But fear not; no matter what path you take,
I (and the dogs) will always track you down.

Scheherazade

Once upon a time
she began, only it wasn't once
and it wasn't that long ago.
She spent the day looking
for dreams she had lost,
names she didn't know,
shapes she didn't need.
She thought everything was real.
She thought everyone waited
to see what she'd say.
But it was just another dream,
a story whose logic had nothing
to do with her, a story
full of thieves, their bandanas
slipped over one eye,
their tongues slippery as swords.
Like songbirds, her hands
flew around her head
as she spoke, they
wrapped turbans or scarves,
whatever the air could imagine.
She wove spells
around their inky hearts,
whispered words for those
she didn't like, even more
for those she did.
She thought she was singing
a song they didn't know,
a song to save her life.
But it was only a dream,
a dream she didn't know

she was dreaming, a dream
where love might be waiting.
Or you. Or you—only you,
one eye open, glittering in the dark.

Tonight, I Dream

A red rhumba
        orange cha-cha
        one-two, one-two-three
perhaps a blue merengue
wild as your hair
        cascading
                like mountain
                        waterfalls
Or a flaming tango
        the scent of mango and coconut
                hovering
in the space between
        our hips, our eyes, our lips.
Tonight, I dream
        a generation
of dreams, time and space
        irrelevant,
a tether of smoke.
        My stars, your stars
my heart your heart
        both beating, both alive
sharing a century between us.
        What matters
is the dance
        the movement into grace.
Here, take my hand. Let go.

Song of the Mattress

After the backaches and sprung
springs, after the tossing and turning,
the hours on the computer, searching,
the days rolling on different beds
which are really all the same beds
with different names in different stores,
after the comparing and the checking
one against the other, the merits
of this one versus that one, the price
points worth the difference (or not),
after the schmoozing and the angst
with the sales staff, the fear I've made
a bad deal, will regret it in a month
maybe two, I finally bought a bed.
Too bad I wasn't this careful with the mate.

Wolf Moon

So close you think collision
is imminent, so large
you could touch it, bring its hard edge
to your mouth, feel the cold
golden glow, like stale ice
stuck to your lip.
This same sense of danger
brings you night after night
to your knees, pliant, postulant,
intemperate in your longing.
planted on this rock, this earth
we call home, baying at moonrise
loudly and alone.
You would think someone
would invite you inside, if only
to give you a tattered bone.

Picking Your Gene Pool

"It must be your genes," I say,
"Dad's family did great."
Silence. Then
"Well, that's a fact," she says.
All my mother's children
have one child who won't leave home.
"It must be my father's family,"
she says, thinking hard. He died
young she told me, while she was a girl.
"My uncle Richard was mean.
His son was a drunk,
raised Catholic, you know.
"What do you suppose it was?"
she asks. I shrug "Who knows?"
thinking that maybe the radicals
are right: there's something to be said
for artificial insemination, picking
each gene like ripe, red fruit.

The Weight of It All

Consider the laws of attraction,
how bound we are—or not.
Caught, convoluted, rotating
in a swirl of galaxies.
It's not a question of gravity,
   though the situation certainly is grave.
More to the point is matter
how light, how dense,
how dark.
  Light, however, travels straight at an absolute
fixed speed, yet seems to bend
the further it gets.
But it's not the light—it's space
  that corners us, hems us in
or expands to prairies full of lonely.
Perception is a zoom lens—
the closer we are, the larger we appear.
   Everything more immediate
like death
when it's ours, and distant
when it's yours.

Faith

And what did Isaac think
when his father took him
by the hand, led him from
his mother's keeping, up
the strange mountain
to the smooth stone table?
What went through his head
as Abraham lifted him up
laid him out, tilted
his neck back just so?
As they trudged back home,
Isaac scrambling to keep up,
do you think it possible
that in his father's presence
he could ever turn his back again?

Transformations

I could be a tree
stump, thick and round
and no one would think
me fat or gnarled
but praise my abundance,
my ringed and knotted bark.
Or a caterpillar
striped and grubby, munching
every milkweed in sight—
eating up admiration for how
I'll transform and fly away.
I could be a mockingbird
singing on a branch,
or an owl hunting mice
or a chameleon eating
mosquitoes and changing
color to hide from sight.
I could be a promise
arcing across a rain-washed sky,
purple and green, blue
and orange into red,
and everyone would stop
and point and smile and sigh.
I could be the sun or the moon
or an exploded star, even a planet
like Saturn, the one I'd like to visit,
maybe just a fly by through its gaseous rings,
its many companions following its orbit.
I could be a virus
replicating itself in a bid
to conquer the world.
Or I could be the cure
for all things evil and cursed.
I could be poetry. I could be life.

Being the Man

Wolves aren't what you expect they are.
They're more: always on the lookout
for the one who's smarter, faster—
not meaner, not sly, not the one in sheep's clothing.
They've gotten a bad rap with tales of pigs
and little girls—sharp canines dripping blood,
heads back, howling in fury, when really
they're only calling like a mother whose child
is dawdling down the block, or for the one
who's taken a wrong turn and is lost.
A real wolf wouldn't bitch slap some woman,
or stray from the pack, wouldn't steal
what didn't belong or eat what wasn't earned.
A real wolf wouldn't wait to be told
who needed protection or what chores
needed doing. Real wolves remember
where they came from, who they are,
and who they've been. A real wolf
doesn't look anything like you.

Hunger

like an alligator
who looks like a log
all day, all night
till a soft plash
sends it leaping
jaws wide, snapping,
all hope for escape
swallowed into the dark maw
of an empty belly.
So, too, the bird
whose weight is measured
in ounces, regretful twigs
snapping like straw
in a summer sun,
whose whole brain fills
with nothing but the hunt:
food, mate, nest.
Like you and I
sizzling in the dark.

Not Only a Hurricane

Each storm has an eye wound tightly
around itself, an empty space
roiling its false calm against a wall
of furious wind, like the tantrum
thrown by a thwarted child
who does not get her way, who never
gets her way, impotent fists pounding
like thunder, eyes flashing like lightning,
the smell of sulfur a sure sign
more trouble's on the way.

Take It On a Wing

in debt to Wallace Stevens

Windy widows we were once,
singing salty songs afloat
like big-beaked birds blackened
in mirrored machinations of absent moons,
or lonely oil spilled on sullied beaches,
like Susanna, syllables spelled like music
in her ears, a red bassoon, beating heart,
disillusioned by unimagined ghosts
white as the sound of snow,
pale as the taste of pears.
But come, comedians, carry me off
she begs, fat as a bantam, cockles
raised in ruinous rhythm, russet
and crepey, like last month's news,
yellowed at the edges, edgy in their tone.
Carry me on currents of air,
blue as breath, blue as a bar,
blue as bare and blue as there,
blue as belly, blue as beam,
blue is whatever I make it seem.
So sayeth she, so sayeth we,
so sayeth all who see
the fiction in the truth, do tell.
Sit still, sit tight, but sing if you will,
and listen in the light of night.
Sunday will not come again.

"Nothing Fits the Body So Well as Water"

—Don DeLillo

Here in this liquid soup
called a Florida night
we swim against the current
of our various angers—this one
slighted by that one—that one
ignored by another—real, imagined,
it matters not. Voices rise
like stalks of corn, their silken tones
now rasped as empty husks,
feelings shucked like so much chaff.
Hold out your hands, let me fill them
with water, watch as you dip
and dip to no avail; it slips away
through the creases of a life worn through.
Lie down in the river, and still
the water rushes around you,
no more than a stone in its path,
never filling it, till you drown.

Redemption

This is about
the spells cast on princesses,
the years they spend asleep.
How they awaken with a jolt
staring straight into the eyes
of some throbbing prince.
But this is not a fairy tale,
it is flesh and sweat.
There is sex and redemption,
violence and rapture.
There is moon and stars and wind,
there is a forest and a Big Bad Wolf.
But the woodcutter has a hard on
and what he hacks is not for love.
There is thunder.
Storms polarize around me
like magnetic dust.
There is lightning and a vision.
There is the endless rain
that falls inside my heart.

Six Poems from the Tang

1. Nee Hao Beijing

>Lions guard gates as Beijing sleeps.
>Dragons chase spirits across the sky,
>Dreams rise like mist.
>Woman sighs, man snores,
>Moon crosses into west.
>Stars blink, close their eyes,
>Sun yawns, roosters crow.

2. Tiananmen Square

>Swallows chase rain drops
>across forbidden square,
>silent wind in my hair.
>Sudden sun startles the sky.
>Roses everywhere.

3. Maid's Lament, Summer Palace

>Willows weep in the wind,
>Star clusters catch in my hair.
>Empress dreams of red.
>Happiness sprinkles like rain.
>I run to the river for fish,
>but my bucket comes up empty.
>Only mistress's words bite!

4. Xi'an

>Pale, long face amidst a sea of round.
>We are all walking, wondering—
>the city a magic dream.
>I smile, they smile, nod
>move on, each life
>now touched
>by my own.

5. Tang Dynasty Dancers

>Embroidered, painted in silk,
>they flow like the river down stage.
>My heart fills with awe,
>flies to their tongue
>comes out a song.

6. Warriors, *Terra Firma*

>*The success of a single general leaves thousands of bodies withered.*
>
>—Cao Song, 879

>To fight for a cause, glorious.
>But who remembers those
>Left standing, whose purpose
>Is only to guard the reviled,
>Not to mention dead?
>I will remember, now,
>Having seen them:
>The soldier, the magicians,
>The archer kneeling with bow.

II. Speaking in Tongues

The Cape Was Never White

—Little Red Riding Hood

First of all, I was not skipping.
I never skip, but yes, I was eating
strawberries: red, ripe, delicious.
I had heard rumors
that girls who ate them
would never want for men.
I was after the woodcutter
not the wolf, but the wolf
was quicker, sly, and intense.
I hadn't meant to enjoy it—
but being swallowed whole
was a definite kick
no man could ever give.

Mrs. Sprat

Young, I was always plump,
Mother carving my body with pills,
curling my hair with perms.
Tuck this here, let that out there,
pads in the bosom of my dress.
Never quite right, the buttons
always strained, the seams always split.
That's how I lost my virginity:
split seams and a kind offer home.
Quick change artist that I was,
I managed to capture a heart.
But dreams wished upon a star
have habits of coming true,
wrap ropes around your neck.
Sill plump, I took what I could get.
It was the sixties, there was plenty
of getting to be had. The dark
hides many things.
A blue-eyed drawl offered revenge,
a dish best eaten cold.
I didn't listen and burned my tongue.
Age turns plump to fat, but still
I had my share: three marriages,
three divorces, a child forever hungry.
Nothing I ever did was safe,
nothing was ever in vain
(except the diets of course), but still
I wound up exactly who I am.

Ahab's Second Wife

After the first one died of regret,
he married me, found
spit up upon a sandless shore,
pale as sea glass, just as hard.
But I was no match for that whale,
his dark dreams full of blubber,
like the first meal he'd fed me,
bit by bit, not a trace of bone or gristle.
You wouldn't think he'd be as tender
but he was, moaned as he came
like some embarrassed woman,
his scar glistening like a fresh bolt from the sky.
Oh, the nights, the nights.
I cherished each one like an oyster's pearl,
my body the only sea he could safely sail,
my hips rocking him to sleep.
Was a time I thought it would be enough,
but no, the tales at the dock, the name
whispered about: "Moby! Moby Dick!"
pulled him harder than my arms could hold him.
When he left that last time
I knew he'd never return. I could smell
the rot in his soul. He handed over his purse,
filled with all he had, but one Spanish eight.
He'd held me all night fixed
in my body like the north star,
rigid as his whale bone stump, still,
like a ship without wind.
It was almost three years before word
finally came; by then, his son
was just past two, his first words learned
from my fevered dreams: "Moby! Moby Dick!"

Sound Over Sense: Miranda's Crisis with Words

Miranda wants to speak
that which can't be spoken;
she needs to empty all the noise,
the voices that shout to thinning air:
There is no moon to shelter stars
no wind to call my name.
Things that take up space
and make sleep a crowded room.

But Miranda's head is filled with words;
the sweet insomnia of lovely sounds
the mystic veil she hides behind.
She doesn't remember that language
means nothing on its own;
speech alone won't solve a thing.
She looks for substance in the reflection of sky.

She needs to find the thread
to sew the holes in night;
her dreams keep falling out.
One by one she picks them up
muttering to the moonless dark:
why can't we see the earth turning?
As if dreams had meaning she could define,
as if gravity didn't exist.

She holds the planets like dandelions
in her hand, blows them away,
then watches where they fall;
she thinks she can put them together
as if nothing has come apart,
as if everything were a puzzle
whose pieces fit in certain shapes,
as if answers had a name.

Miranda's Fairy Tale

Miranda has had a number of lovers.
Not all of them good, or even
remarkable in any way except
for the chance they might have had.

She often wondered what honey
clung to the scent of her skin
to bring so many of them
hunting her flesh.

And when they'd gone, she wondered
if the bees sucked her dry
or the bears had pawed it all,
deserted as an empty hive.

The air would thicken with orange scent,
Miranda, restless as a butterfly
strengthened by winter's retreat,
would begin to breathe again.
Sloe-eyed, she would creep among
tangled vines clinging for support
and stumble into the arms
of another would-be prince.

Miranda had kissed a lot of frogs,
none of whom had changed much,
and one final day she knew
what she'd been doing wrong.

There was a trick in not looking,
forget the ermine and gold,
the feel of velvet skin,
and never, never wear lilies.

Coming to Terms

Miranda married for love.
In itself, that's not unusual
but in Miranda's case
there was more to be considered.
She needed someone to love
her while she wasn't sure
what the word really meant.

She sometimes thought it meant
the same as need,
but needs change so often
it didn't seem practical.
She'd already had three
and couldn't imagine too many more,
though marriage and forever
certainly weren't the same.

Other times she thought it was friendship,
the physical aspect only a way
of relieving the tension of being close,
a kind of reflex action,
conditioned response.

Miranda's mind clouded like a summer
storm, a black wind which blew
from the past and left acceptance
like puddles in her path.
She decided not to question nature.

Nothing is forever. It simply
goes until it ends.
The distance is irrelevant.
Miranda wondered if she had a defect
in spatial comprehension.

Miranda in Her First Short Poem

Miranda is swimming upstream,
her lungs about to burst.
She knows why she does it
but pretends she doesn't.

If she stops to think
she will drown
so she doesn't stop
and she doesn't drown.

Instead she swims on
thinking there's a destination,
a logical end
to this endless swimming.

How odd life is, full
of surprises. Miranda
takes a deep breath
and goes back down.

If you look closely,
catch a certain light,
you can see her smile,
red mouth, tiny silver bubbles.

"Dance Without Sleeping"

—from Never Enough, *Melissa Ethridge*

Miranda loves to dance,
to close her eyes and sway
to the rhythms in her head.
She likes to feel her body
moving, its fluid grace
a contradiction to her daily
clumsiness, as if walking
were just too ordinary
to be given much thought.

She loves to gyrate her hips,
watch them naked in the mirror,
imagine the bones and sockets
as they slide beneath her skin;
then she'll spin, feeling the bones
in her feet, rising up
on the balls, coming down
gradually, cushioned by her
gently bending toes, so effortless.

Her arms raise and lower,
she lifts her hair, shakes
her head, the music
her master, she a puppet.
The blue drums,
red sax, hummingbirds
caught in her chest,
waiting for their chance to fly.

Permeable Truths

Miranda likes to say she's honest
and she is—to a point.
Emotional honesty, she says
begins and ends with self.
It has little to do with anyone else,
what is told or not told,
known or not known,
as long as she knows the truth.

And she does, even though she tries
to push it back under her skirts,
pretend it's not there, squirming
and wriggling like an earthworm in love.
Miranda sits back in her big chair
and composes her stories: the official one,
the semi-official one for closer friends,
and the real one for herself.

She realizes the danger, however,
blinking like Bob's Barricades
loudly in the night; how truth
can grow faint, begins to blend
with the stories, until one day
when the sun is especially bright
or the moon uncommonly full,
they are one truth—and all lies.

Miranda Confesses Idolatry

Miranda has a confession
she is loath to make.
Out building naves, little altars
of names, small kindnesses
she collects like relics,
words she reads in the dark—
she knows how she looks.
Ridiculous becomes me, she says
to anyone who listens.
Under the moon too long,
her skin is burned white ash.

She knows what she's doing,
dancing from town to town
chasing icons, another candle lit.
She likes the flame, the blue center,
creamy tip, a hint of red only
where the wick has tasted fire.
She likes to watch it flicker, imagines
it moves to the music in her head.
Kneeling in front of her shrines,
Miranda prays for gifts,
talent rubbed in the palms of her hands.

Poetry is like rain, she thinks:
the sky opens and it falls.

Miranda Contemplates Silence

sees a tornado, a hurricane,
whatever winds tightly around dead space.
The roar turns her deaf,
a muffled sea lapping gently
at the shores of her skin.

She's been told silence is healing
tries to imagine destruction
reconstructing itself, like in cartoons,
flattened buildings spring back,
trees and people unbend and stand tall.

She might even *like* the quiet, grow
used to the sounds of her body,
the rhythms of blood and bone,
if it weren't for the violence,
that initial shock of assault—
and the walls. Everywhere
she looks, there are walls.

Miranda as Mermaid

Miranda stepped off the boat in mid-ocean.
Those who saw would later claim
her walk had purpose, direction;
she knew what she was doing.

She had seen the mountains
in the sea, salt crags caked green,
caves of creatures still called fish;
the heights made her dizzy.

The caves were first, dark and full,
watery apparitions that loomed
like black clouds, eels flashing
long bright threads through rock.

Miranda swam on, her body
charged with force of wave,
tidal currents of electro-shock,
the undulations of instinct.

She reached the base of the tallest peak
dressed in seaweed strands
floating weightless as in space
close to the lunar pull.

Miranda began to climb, hands cut
on the shell of eons of coral
living on top of their past
creating the presence of future.

Without pickax, rope, or provision
she inched the stony surface,
laughter in her lungs,
madness an exhilaration of sorts.

At the top, Miranda bubbled loud,
poked her head above the wave,
saw the ship in a bottle,
smiled and returned home.

Pondering Stones and Their Relation to Mathematics

Miranda is still getting lost.
She's always had a problem
negotiating space, bumping
into this or that, aware
only at night finding blue
and purple bruises
scattered like islands
over her body.

It's her own fault. She wanders
dark tunnels and convoluted paths,
too much in her heart
some of the time, the rest in her head.
She can't read the signs;
selective dyslexia, she calls it,
where the letters spell something else.

Miranda thinks maybe she should study physics,
learn how to order the universe
on specific spatial planes,
or perhaps calculus, a new language
of symbolic notation, a method
for predicting variables both known and unknown.
Perhaps then she'd find her way out
of the geometric dead end of circles.

Seance

Miranda must go a long way
inside herself to discover the inner
labyrinths, the ones she hasn't time
to explore, has only heard about—
mystical catacombs
in the basement of her mind.

She wonders what she should pack:
a coat of mail, quill-tipped pen
with indelible ink, the heart-
shaped box her mother gave her
more than twenty years ago.
It's important, she decides, to be well prepared.

Right now, she's hunting for a candle
thinking it's the proper light
for explorations in the dark,
the smell of tallow, hot wax
dripping down her hand,
a full moon and a stiff wind.

Miranda closes her eyes, takes
a deep breath and descends.
The stairs are steep and wind
in oddly random patterns.
A golden luminescence clings
to her body, darkness beyond.

She wishes she'd brought a torch.
At the bottom, she stops, sits down,
places the candle before her
and waits—is there, waiting still.
See? Just inside this door. Knock
once for "yes," twice for "no."

Contemplating Kafka and the Fate of Gregor

Miranda's been running in circles
up, over, around, under everyone
she meets, like one of those steam rollers
you see everywhere these days,
every city getting new streets
with all of us caught in the jam.
But this isn't about streets
unless it's those long, dark ones,
winding further and further
into the scrub pine, the forests
we don't go into, the ones
that sprout at nothing more
than a dead end.
It's not as if she doesn't know it,
can't see herself as she races
from project to project, like the way she cooks,
all the dishes going at the same time,
stirring here, slicing there.
She watches herself all the time.
She's tried to change,
at least she's thought about it—
chided herself for being too blunt,
too talkative, too self-centered—
all the adjectives for over-bearing,
but Miranda has no time.
She needs space to script a life,
find a role to emulate,
make new costumes, shape
new masks, paint and feather,
try them on, rehearse,
feel comfortable again.

Perhaps a Southern sensibility,
all slow honey in its own sweet time,
a long drawl that demands attention,
deliberate pace, as if weighty, thinking.
Miranda tries on white gloves,
but prefers her raw, hard hands.

Northern intellectual, she thinks,
long sweaters and glasses,
enroll in post-doctoral work,
go for a Ph.D. in Comparative Lit.,
a Fulbright to Albania,
read critical reviews for fun.

But she's already myopic,
and she doesn't speak Albanian.
She is what she is:
a transplanted Midwesterner
living in a southern town
that thinks it's not.

Romancing the Numbers

Miranda, naked, sits cross-legged on the bed.
She is loving a man with her eyes only
because he does not exist. She has made him
up in her mind and he is the perfect lover.
His kisses cover her body, reach every crevice,
shed new light on darkness.

Miranda rocks back and forth and shakes her head,
counting beats of her heart. She is practicing Love
in the Perfumed Garden, the Arabic way.
She is on number fourteen and by the time
she reaches twenty-five, she will die of ecstasy.
She knows this and does not mind.

"Desire is the wish for heaven," she says,
her hands fluttering like hummingbirds
around her body. She feels them peck and bite,
knows the power of suggestion.
What, after all, is reality, but a different spatial plane,
a riddle we move to, traveling in circles?

It is not the answer, she thinks, that binds us,
it is the question unasked—
the one where purpose is not a definition
but an adventure yet to be had.
Miranda sighs, lies down and closes her eyes.
Her lover sleeps, then brings her gently to fifteen.

III. An Asylum of Cuckoos

A Tidings of Magpies

Never do they bring any luck
or love or money, never good will.
Harbingers of woe.

Gossip, gossip, gossip.
Rumors are rarely still.
Never do they bring any luck

Magpies are smart, social,
feast on what others kill.
Harbingers of woe.

To a magpie, everything is black and white,
no grey lines to cross or fill,
never do they bring any luck.

Magpies know themselves,
clearly peck in mirrors, their ebony bills
harbingers of woe.

Listen to their song, since you never know
where they've been or the stories they'll tell.
Never do they bring any luck.
Harbingers of woe.

A Waddle of Penguins

No longer marching. Marching
is for the young ones, looking
to mate. No, "waddle" is perfect
describing the never limber limbs
sliding awkwardly around
as if they thought
they had somewhere to go.

A Parliament of Owls

Which came first?
Parliament or owls? No doubt
the white wigged men
in government were thought
to be wise, but really, the owl
was first, Athena's crest in gold.

Who—who whoever the namer was,
St. Albans in his book on hunting—15th century—
or some literary type seeing a simile
between members of Parliament
and touchy, screechy owls startled
to the rafters, no one seems to know.

Visualize this: Barn owls, burrowing owls,
snowy owls, over 200 types of owls—
all bickering and hunting, claiming their space,
their territory, congressing together.
Sound familiar? Watch closely.
See how they vote.

A Descent of Woodpeckers

Drum roll, please: introducing
the Red Bellied Woodpecker
whose head, not his belly is red.
Lovelorn, he'll hammer for hours
on some unlucky tree already dying
from blight or frustrated peckers
who never got an answer.

It seems females of all species
wait a day or two, even a week
to return a call, and when they do,
what a racket! Not your best
boy band drummer
but still, the call is made.
Old chisel tip
digs holes in trees for a nest,
then shows it to his girl—
if she likes him, she'll hop right in,
make herself comfy, then head
for the nearest moss
to gather better bedding.

Watch him circle their nest
high in the sky, then drop like lead
to catch an ant, showing off
his sticky prowess, his tongue
like a rake, filling his beak.
Proudly, he hops to his mate,
opens his mouth and shows her
his wonderful, wriggling catch.
Satisfied, she lays her eggs
and soon, her nestlings hatch.

It's an age-old story, the birds and the bees,
but bees aren't needed here, so . . .
The male will stick around till
the hatchlings fly, even help feed them,
but soon as he can, he's off looking
(and so is she). Serial monogamy.
Seems to work. We should give it a try.

A Murder of Crows

When the birds fly at sunset
from wire to wire, sweeping
in harmony, lifted wing,
they most likely will be crows
or their cousins, the grackle.
The crows' yellow eyes fix on their fellows,
seeing the signals out of the corners
of their vision, swooping up, down
across, then land, each moving over
to give room to the other as it grips the wire.

The name, it seems, comes from their propensity
for gathering at death, a funeral, last rites, farewell
to the flock, a number minus one or two.
They aren't given to murder one another,
though it is not entirely alien if one oversteps.
Perhaps they're investigating a crime scene,
maybe an accident, one bird whose wings touched
another on the line and fried, falling to earth.

How do they, we, grieve our losses?
In public or in private matters not, it's grief
nonetheless; a lesson learned. Come dawn,
all voices will rise again.

An Unkindness of Ravens

When the ravens scattered seeds
that grew into people, perhaps
they were of evil intent, knowing
the havoc men would create.

Some say they are witches, disguised
as any living thing, hiding in plain sight,
adorned with thick, feathered collars,
able to speak in human voices.
Perhaps those poor, unfortunates
who seem to have lost their minds
are really following orders given by a raven.

When Poe heard his raven speak
"nevermore" its answers were perfectly
in tune to his grief, the darkness
in his wounded heart.
Ravens are cunning, deceitful,
tricking each other as well as people.

No soul, no heart, no remorse.
When a raven croaks his tailored message,
take heed: it may well be
the last thing you ever hear.

A Flamboyance of Flamingoes

Florida is known for many things:
heat, humidity, hurricanes.
Of course, there are seagulls, storks,
palm trees, and yes, flamingoes
who live mostly in parks, protected
from poachers, which makes me wonder
if our other flamboyant residents need protecting, too.
We have bars, restaurants, theaters, clubs, festivals.
They come wearing flamingo hats, shirts, Hawaiian shorts,
flip flops and painted toenails, as bright as any bird.

Baby flamingoes are not born flamboyant,
but grey or white, fed milk by their mothers
who spit it up and into their tiny beaks.
Depending on what they later eat,
the birds turn pink or red, even orange
and stay close to home, monogamous, content.
Though there are often thousands
in a flock, they are usually in small groups.
As any breeder knows, numbers are good for diversity,
though a shrinking pool is not good for anyone,
bird or beast or man.

An Asylum of Cuckoos

Surrogate parenting is nothing new.
Cuckoo birds have done it forever.
The eggs the females lay in seconds flat
have even evolved as look-alikes
to the warbler or magpie
whose home she commandeered.

She doesn't even wait
for an empty nest but settles
right in, shoving its occupant over,
then flies off to mate and repeat,
up to fifty eggs a season.

This profligate isn't all bad, though:
she often waits in a nearby tree
making sure her offspring are hatched, then fed.
The weird thing is those changelings
cry so loud, any flying bird might drop a caterpillar
in their mouths, for the sake of forest peace.

And the hatchlings? No wren or lark loyalty for them!
They fly off soon as they can and drop their eggs
wherever, while the hapless male, dazed and confused
by all his one-night stands, does nothing but fly
through the night repeating his name, perhaps
an admonishment for his risky behavior.
Or a strong case for nature over nurture.

A Wake of Vultures

What more is there to say?
Let's eat!

A Mob of Emus

It's all over the news—
mobs of displaced people from Venezuela,
Serbia, Guatemala, Honduras, Israel,
Parkland: students, parents, police,
people everywhere surging toward
something, a goal, a purpose, a dream.

For the emu, thousands in a flock, it's different.
They know exactly what they're after and they run,
not fly, to get it: food, water, stones to grind
food in their gullets, females to lay the eggs,
males to sit the nest, raise the young.

It's an intriguing switch, males as caregivers.
The female roams from nest to nest
male to male, leaving her green eggs behind.
Her intensely wide, amber eyes dare you
to judge her, her long, emerald neck,
her legs built to run, always running.
A mob of emus, who could peck your eyes out,
open a hole in your head; don't get in the way.

Once the agitation is started, the mob takes over
dusting up anyone in its path,
same as the people who think they're running
for freedom, home, someplace else,
or for no reason at all, just because they can.
Never mind there's a river, a forest, a wall.

A Murmurration of Starlings

Think young stars
streaking across the night sky
or an alien from a distant land
whose sun might be newer
or more ancient than our own.

Had it not been for Shakespeare
inspiring fevered minds with birds,
the starlings might have remained
in Europe, but America
had to have them and now
they're a pestilence, a scourge
of millions darkening midday in swarms,
murmuring incessantly their secrets
to anyone who will listen.

Thousands, even millions in a flock
block the sun; perhaps this is
what caused the last great extinction,
the darkness and noise driving even
the dinosaurs mad, plants withering,
the water fouled, the world gone to rot.

Regardless, mankind
is always the cause, out of arrogance
or misbegotten plans, and now
in this Anthropocene era, perhaps
we, along with the starlings
will fly off into the blazing sunset
never looking back, never seen again.

A Kettle of Hawks

Double trouble, boil and bubble . . .
Watch out when the hawks circle 'round.
Swoop and dive, claws that catch, carry
off into the night their prey.

No gentle scarf or hood protects you,
no cloak or dagger, no scattered shot.
Too swift, too dark, too sharp, too far.
Look anywhere but in their eye.

Cross the road, the field, the stony path,
hide between the trees. Cover your tracks.
Shun the moon, the sun, the stars,
do not be led astray.

Listen hard, look between the clouds,
duck and cover, run, run, run,
and never, never trip.
Your fall will be goodbye.

A Skein of Geese

We might learn from geese
who mate for life,
winging their way south
to raise their young
in warmer climes, then fly
back north in summer.
Their plump formations
against the sun and sky
cause farmers to stop their work
and marvel at the flock.
The hunters double up.

A Quarrel of Sparrows

From window to window
across the rooftops,
hear them argue!
It doesn't matter
who's right or wrong,
insults flung, words hang
in the air like rotting fish.

You think your neighbors are loud,
vulgar, like the hundreds of sparrows
whose bickering in the eaves
settles like an earworm
and all you ever hear
is their cacophony of chirps.

Some think sparrows are ill omens,
ferrying souls to heaven, so many in a flock
pestering the skies, dirtying the streets.

But Aphrodite adored the sparrow,
made it a symbol of love—
makes sense, since lovers so often quarrel—
but perhaps it was the extra bone in their tongues
that Aphrodite admired, good for more
than breaking seeds.

A Squad of Pelicans

The pelicans line up like old soldiers—
balding at the pate, rheumy eyes,
sharp beaks smelling something fishy
blocks away.

They stand in rows on piers,
seawalls, benches, breathing
heavily through their mouths.
When they're hungry, they fly
off over the water, dive down
and scoop their dinner
into their mouths, gulping
as fast as they can.

The pelican harkens back thirty
million years, giving nuance
to the phrase "tough old bird."
It's also why they're not eaten.

At sunset, you can see them saluting
each other, a scrawny wing raised
to the sky, their webby feet unbound
by shoe or boot or fishing line.
See how they fly straight into the sun.

A Deceit of Lapwings

Lies! Fake news! You can't believe
what you read or watch,
as Someone will tell you
you didn't see what you saw.

An apt alternative name is "peewit"
and anyone who is looking can see
the resemblance to a certain Someone,
especially in the crest on top of its head.

In ancient Egypt, lapwings were symbolic
of the kings atop the downtrodden people
and were crafty at hiding their homes
from those who wish them harm.

The hatchlings are in such a hurry
they leave the nest with pieces of shell
attached to their heads, and run off
at the mouth without warning or care.

The sound they make is "weep weep!"
as though we needed another occasion for tears.

A Charm of Finches

I'm a finch. Not just any bird
but a Gouldian Finch.
Yes, you can admire my brilliance
in color and brains but hands off!
I don't like to be handled.
You want a hop on hop off-er,
get a parakeet who screeches,
not a quiet one like me
who speaks when there's something to say
and needs lots of room to fly.

Why we're called a "charm"
I've no idea, as being blunt
is not my most charming trait.
But there you have it:
Look as much as you like,
admire our grace in flight,
our cute little social chirps,
but don't be surprised
if we bite the hand that feeds us.

A Scold of Jays

Out walking the dog at dusk,
I heard a racket of blue jays
in a tree, screaming and flying
in and out of the branches.

A Burrowing owl swooped
into the foliage and out,
clutching a baby jay in its claws.
After that, only the silence
of the falling night.

Blue jays aren't actually blue
but a soft brown with pockets of air
fluffing their feathers toward the light.
Thus, the illusion of blue.

We all tend to accept illusions.
like safety and protection, but even
when the jays disguise their voices
into hawks or even humans,
no one is fooled, and are prey
to every living thing stronger
and faster, hungrier than the noisy jay,
who will divebomb anything
if it gets too close to their nest.

Protection is an inborn instinct,
and all of us seem to use whatever means
necessary, even if we don't always succeed.

A Piteousness of Doves

Pigeons, doves—can't tell
one from another—they all look alike,
sound alike, too, with their soft stutters,
relentless echoing coos.

They can be short or tall,
thin or fat, but still
they look alike—pestilence in feathers,
clogging skies, roofs, borders.

What's to be done? Cage the sky?
"Keep them out! Don't feed them!"
People shout, pointing arms toward the sun.
No wonder doves try to soothe
with their gentle murmur, hopeful
and piteous all at the same time.

A Herd of Cranes

It's not impossible to imagine the crane,
with its graceful dance and haunting song,
the elaborate head pumps and wings flapping
inspiring those artful Japanese prints.
All the cranes are faithful birds, good companions,
sacred and protected the world over.
A crane in your yard symbolizes longevity, good fortune,
and a folded paper crane brings peace and happiness.

Never underestimate the power of a dance or a song
to move even the most stubborn of creatures.
Migrating cranes fly over deserts and mountains,
thousands of miles to find the best mates,
hopping, twisting, turning in a mad dance of love.
Whoever named them a herd must never have tried,
for herding cranes is like herding cats—
who everyone knows refuse to obey orders.

A Pandemonium of Parrots

Each afternoon around five
a dozen parrots fly overhead
squawking their wild freedom
to anyone in earshot.
It's chaos, as other birds
startle from their nests
and fly for different shelter,
their panicked chirps adding
to the pandemonium above.

These green, speechless parrots
are jailbirds from the zoo,
having escaped in a hurricane.
They've migrated over the years
to neighborhoods north and south,
though no one really knows
where they nest, only their overhead flights
and their infernal racket.

It's said that parrots, once free,
are seldom ever caught.

A Watch of Nightingales

I have always been stone cold deaf, my love
and more than a little alone, my love.

And though I can't sing a jaunty tune
I can groan "starry starry night," my love.

In the sunlight, the vowels dance, fly
like blind butterflies blown by wind, my love.

If I were young and limber like before,
I'd buy letters whose sounds bend and moan, "my love."

Strung together like a chain of daisies,
Words rain in color, then are thrown, my love.

Poetry's a song I don't need to sing
Words are spoken, then they're sown, my love.

I don't sleep at night, and like a singing
watch of nightingales, now I've flown, my love.

About the Author

Barbra Nightingale has six chapbooks and two previous volumes of poetry with small presses. She is an Associate Editor with the South Florida Poetry Journal, a professor emerita from Broward College, and lives in Hollywood, Florida, with her two- and four-legged menagerie. She is completing work on her first memoir, *Husbands and Other Strangers*.

Other Books by the Author

Lovers Never Die (1981)

Prelude to a Woman (1986)

Lunar Equations (1993)

Singing in the Key of L (1999)

Greatest Hits (2000)

The Ex-Files (2005)

Geometry of Dreams (2009)

Two Voices One Past (2010)

Alphalexia (2019)

www.ingramcontent.com/pod-product-compliance
Lightning Source LLC
Chambersburg PA
CBHW032236080426
42735CB00008B/883